The Heritage Collection

KING OSEI TUTU I
FOUNDER OF THE ASANTE EMPIRE

Letitia deGraft Okyere

Illustrated by Masum Ahmed

Lion's Historian PRESS
Amplifying Authentic Voices

King Osei Tutu I: Founder of the Asante Empire
Copyright © 2025 by Letitia deGraft Okyere

Illustrator: Masum Ahmed
Layout designer: Nasim Malik Sarkar

Library of Congress Control Number: 2025908000

All rights reserved.

No part of this publication may be reproduced, stored in a retrieval system, a database, and/or published in any form or by any means, electronic, mechanical, photocopying, recording or otherwise, without the prior written permission of the publisher.

ISBN 978-1-956776-28-7 hardcover
ISBN 978-1-956776-29-4 ebook

Published by Lion's Historian Press
https://www.lionshistorian.net/

For

Kofi, Nana, and Kwabena Okyere

A Brief Introduction

In the thirteenth century, Akans are believed to have migrated from the southern edges of the Sahara Desert, now Mali, to Techiman in present-day Ghana. Differences between the various Akan clans led to separation. Fante-speaking Akans traveled downwards from Techiman toward the coast and settled there. The Twi-speaking Akans, who were hunters, rejected the coast and made their way to Adanse. Adanse was rich in gold with fertile lands, benefitting from the Ofin, Oda, and Pra rivers.

Clans started moving away from Adanse in the early 1600s. Migrations increased when the Agona clan defeated neighbors in the Adanse area and established the powerful Kingdom of Denkyira. As Denkyira expanded, life became unbearable for non-Agona clans in Adanse. By 1629, fierce disputes and scarcity of farming and hunting land pressed the need for separation from Denkyira. Some migrants traveled northward, creating towns or villages collectively known as Amanse.

The Oyoko clan, a breakaway from the Ekuona clan, left Adanse to establish states like Asantemanso, Kokofu, Nsuta, and Dwaben. Oti Akenten moved the Oyoko clan to Kwaman and assimilated other clans. To build loyalty, Oti Akenten gave leaders of newly merged clans positions of power and influence. For example, Adu Gyamfi, from a town close to Kwaman, became Oti Akenten's

Gyaasehene (or head of the king's household). Obiri Yeboa succeeded Oti Akenten and Adu Gyamfi was regent after Obiri Yeboa's death until Osei Tutu I ascended to the throne. Osei Tutu I, an Oyoko, followed the path of his maternal uncles and sought to transform Kwaman into a strong state.

Contents

Chapter 1: Osei Tutu I's Ancestors 1
Chapter 2: Birth of a King 5
Chapter 3: A Hostage in Denkyira 9
Chapter 4: Lessons at Denkyira's Court 11
Chapter 5: Living in Akwamu 15
Chapter 6: Osei Tutu I is King 19
Chapter 7: Early Victories 23
Chapter 8: Coalition Building 27
Chapter 9: War with Denkyira 31
Chapter 10: The Asante Constitution 35
Chapter 11: The Great King Dies 39
Chapter 12: King Osei Tutu I's Legacy 43

Glossary 47
Quiz 50
References 51
Fun Fact About the Asante 54
Other Books in the Heritage Collection 55

CHAPTER 1

Osei Tutu I's Ancestors

Osei Tutu I's lineage may be traced back to Ankyewaa Nyame, the shared Oyoko ancestress. Historians write that Ankyewaa Nyame was Osei Tutu I's maternal great-great-grandmother. Due to war in Adanse, Ankyewaa Nyame and her daughter, Birepomaa Piesie — meaning a great woman and first-born of her mother — resettled in Asantemanso, close to Asumengya. Birepomaa Piesie had ten children and in the early years, her sons, Osei Tutu I's great uncles, Akyampon Tenten first, followed by twin brothers, Twum and Antwi, ruled over the family.

Kwabia Anwanfi, Osei Tutu I's uncle and Birepomaa Piesie's grandson, succeeded Antwi around 1610. Kwabia Anwanfi was displeased with Asantemanso and sent a hunter to search for a new dwelling place. The hunter found a fertile *afuo* (or farm) owned by a man called Kokor and reported back. Kwabia Anwanfi visited many times before making his home at Kokor's afuo (or Kokofu). As Kwabia Anwanfi settled in Kokofu with close family, other descendants of Birepomaa Piesie established places like Nsuta and Dwaben.

Close to 1644, another of Osei Tutu I's maternal uncles, Oti Akenten, succeeded Kwabia Anwanfi. Just before Oti Akenten became head of the family, Osei Tutu I's aunt traveled through Kwaman to visit her husband and enjoyed the weather. On her return to Kokofu, she told Oti Akenten about it. Oti Akenten

went to Kwaman to explore the area. Oti Akenten agreed the weather was pleasant and was even more delighted when he discovered that the small hills bordering Kwaman served as a natural defense against invaders. In addition, Kwaman's swampy areas were impossible to cross during the rainy season. Oti Akenten bargained with the residents and purchased a piece of land because he had no desire to settle on property owned by others.

Over the next few years, other clans moved to Kwaman, and their differences caused infighting. A council of leaders agreed to appoint Oti Akenten ruler of this new nation at Kwaman, whereas before, he was the king of his clan only, as with his predecessors, from Akyampon Tenten to Kwabia Anwanfi. By the end of King Oti Akenten's reign around 1679, he had defeated neighboring states, adding more territory to Kwaman. Asante folklore tells that King Oti Akenten's name comes from his expansion plans, *Oti, a wagye oman akenten so,* i.e., Oti who formed a nation with land from all over. King Oti Akenten laid the foundation for Osei Tutu I's reign over Kwaman and Asante.

Osei Tutu I's Ancestry

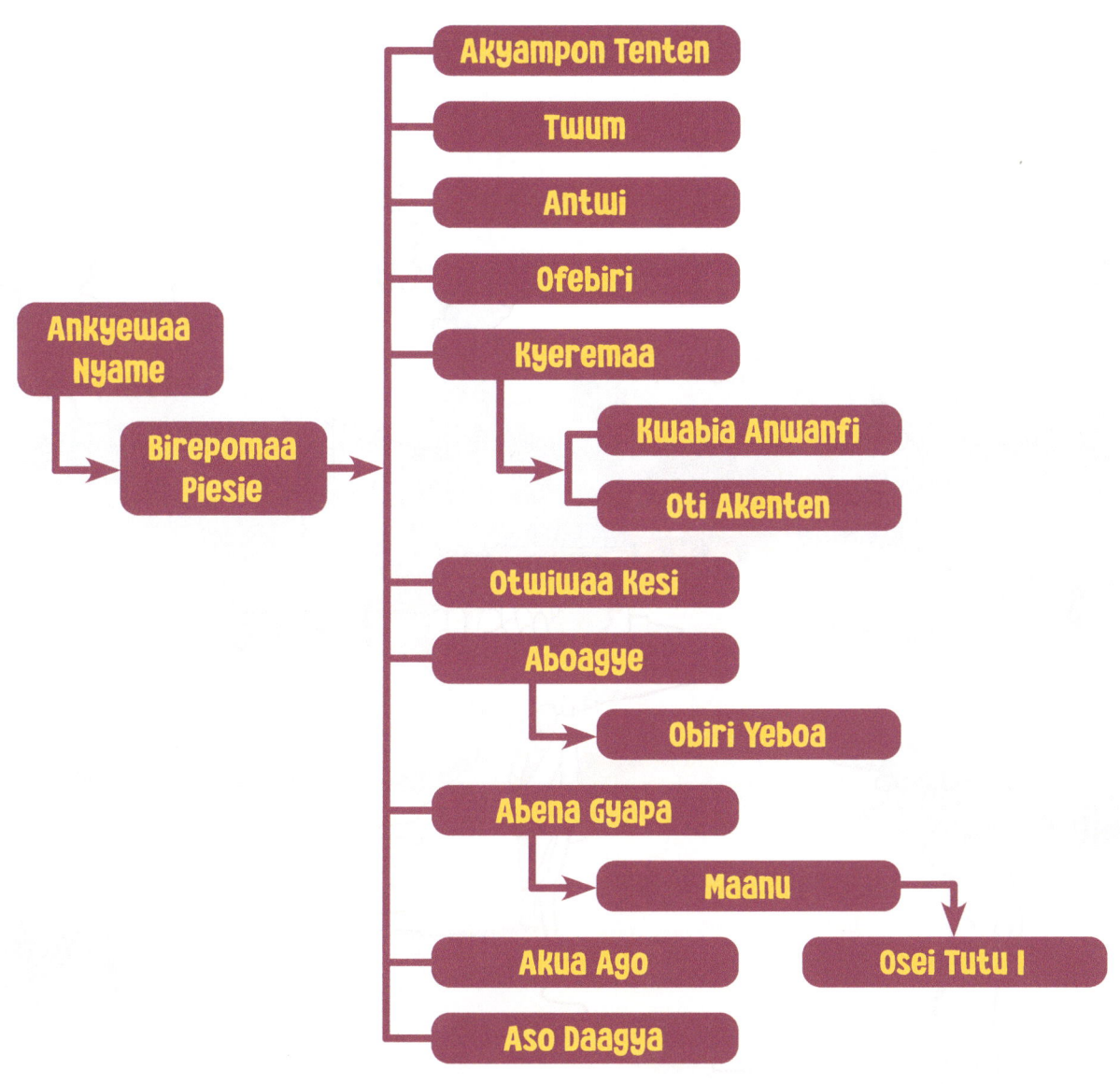

CHAPTER 2

Birth of a King

Osei Tutu I's mother, Maanu Kotosii, and Oti Akenten were great-grandchildren of Ankyewaa Nyame. Thus, in the Akan tradition of matrilineal lineage, they were considered siblings even though they had different mothers. Osei Tutu I's father was Owusu Panin, chief of a small city-state close by. The Kwaman Oyoko family approved of Maanu's marriage to Owusu Panin because it helped with King Oti Akenten's expansion plans.

Maanu and her husband, Owusu Panin, remained childless. This worried her brothers because it left the Oyoko Kwaman throne without an heir. The family sent Maanu away to seek help. She obtained the blessings of a priest in a neighboring state and became pregnant soon after her return to Kwaman. When Maanu's due date grew close, she went to Kokofu to be with her mother. Maanu's son, Osei Tutu I, was born under a silk cotton tree in the 1660s, during King Oti Akenten's reign.

As was the custom, he was bathed by his grandmother with a *sapɔ* (or sponge) made from the stem of a *Momordica*, beaten to a pulp. When the sponge was no longer needed, it was thrown away. It took root, growing into a large tropical climbing plant, predicting that Maanu's son would be a man of enormous influence. After the birth of her son Osei Tutu I, Maanu had two daughters, Bimma Fita and Kyiroma, ensuring that the throne remained within the family.

The young child Osei Tutu I grew up at the palace observing court protocol. As an heir to the throne, his mother and uncles gave him the necessary training to know how to lead. Osei Tutu I received lessons in the art of war; King Oti Akenten instilled the need to enlarge the borders of the state. If Kwaman grew to include areas producing kola nuts and trade routes, the state's wealth and military strength would increase.

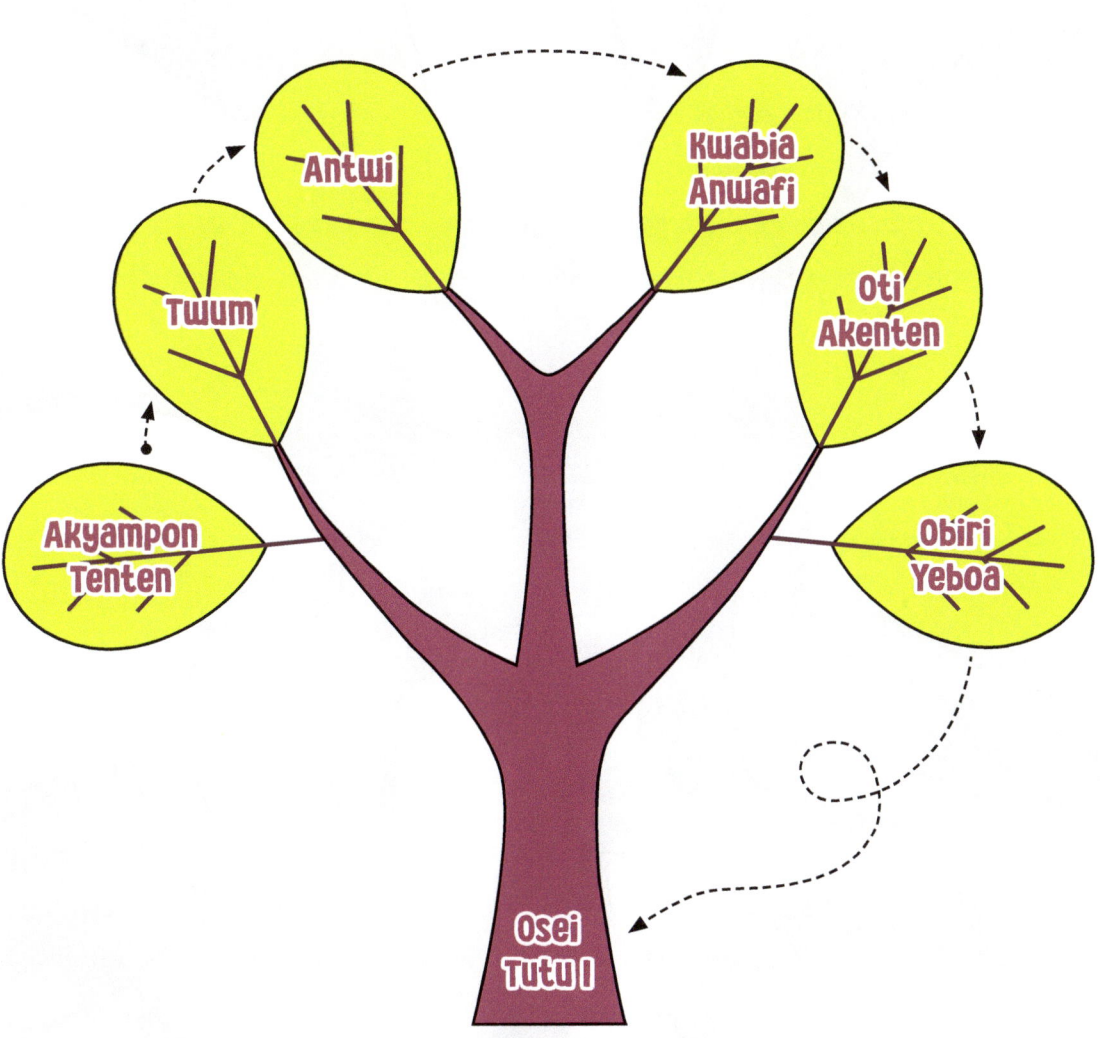

CHAPTER 3

A Hostage in Denkyira

When Osei Tutu I was in his teens, he served King Boa Amponsem of Denkyira in his capital city of Abankeseso. Denkyira was lord over many states, including Kwaman. In years past, states in the region dared to war against Denkyira and lost. Denkyira had gained wealth by trading gold and kola nut, and strength through military conquest. Denkyira kings were feared and earned the nickname, *Menesono*, i.e., those who swallow elephants.

After the defeat, Kwaman and other vassal states sent yearly tributes of palm to King Boa Amponsem. Denkyira kings demanded that subject states send royal heirs to reside at Abankeseso for an indefinite period. King Oti Akenten selected Osei Tutu I to satisfy this requirement. Denkyira believed that an heir's presence gave the vassal state a reason to avoid rebellion, assuring obedience and loyalty. After an heir returned home and ascended to the throne, he would remember how well he was treated, building peaceful relations with his overlord.

Though a captive of Denkyira, Osei Tutu I was treated as the king's guest. He was trained in royal protocol and moved about freely. Osei Tutu I saw other advantages to his stay in Denkyira. He would learn how the different branches of government worked and seek to understand its military strategies. A Denkyira soldier knew no retreat, fighting until death. This knowledge, applied to Kwaman would create a path out of its vassal status.

CHAPTER 4

Lessons at Denkyira's Court

While Osei Tutu I was in Denkyira, he discovered the qualities of the kingdom. Unlike the other Akan states, Denkyira had sacred unifying objects like a stool made from precious beads and a special ceremonial sword. Musicians showered appellations telling of the sharp-quilled porcupine who was Denkyira's subject. Abankeseso was a center for trade because of its skilled and varied craftsmen.

Osei Tutu I studied laws, court procedures, and mannerisms expected of nobility. He witnessed Denkyira's trade patterns with Europeans and how the state built up its supply of ammunition and weapons that made Denkyira's military feared in the region. He appreciated the benefit of Denkyira's trading relationships with both the natives — at the Begho market to the north — and the Europeans, along the coast, to the south. At the Denkyira court, Osei Tutu I sat with King Boa Amponsem to receive delegations of Europeans laden with gifts. He became the king's shield bearer because of his contributions. Osei Tutu I enjoyed social activities with members of the royal family, skillful at games like oware. He also earned the respect of the people of Denkyira.

However, the handsome and strong Osei Tutu I overstepped his boundaries when he had a relationship with Princess Bensua, the sister of King Boa Amponsem. He was a mere nephew of a vassal king making the relationship

forbidden. In addition, Princess Bensua had been promised in marriage to an important associate of the king. Osei Tutu I faced execution for treason. He fled Abankeseso for his life, traveling eastward because he could not return home. King Boa Amponsem would have poured his vengeance on Kwaman for giving refuge to Osei Tutu I. The heir to the Kwaman throne now had to seek an ally strong enough to withstand the might of Denkyira.

CHAPTER 5

Living in Akwamu

Osei Tutu I went to Akwamu, another rising Akan state north of Accra, the capital city of present-day Ghana. He sought protection from the *Akwamuhene* (or King of Akwamu). This was a good strategy because Akwamu and Denkyira were enemies. Also, with the King of Akwamu's desire to enlarge his borders, he saw a benefit in forming a bond with the heir to Kwaman's throne. At the very least, if Kwaman went to war against Akyem, northwest of Akwamu, this would free Akwamu to push its boundaries further east. Akyem remained a rival and a threat to Akwamu's plans.

In Akwamu, Osei Tutu I studied the political and social structures of this centralized state with one supreme leader. The King of Akwamu had established trading arrangements with the Dutch, Danish, and English posts in the region. Osei Tutu I was keen to learn how Akwamu bargained with the Europeans to obtain needed supplies including firearms. He was comparing Akwamu and Denkyira trade patterns.

Life in Akwamu was much like what he had known in Denkyira, with the liberty to travel among its vassal states. Osei Tutu I traded in gold and other items while deepening his ties with Akwamu. Osei Tutu I was hardworking and charming, and the king gave him the honor of Akwamuhene's ɔkra i.e., the king's soul mate. At this time, Osei Tutu I met with a court priest, Kwame

Agyei Firempong, and they became friends. The court priest would become an important member of Osei Tutu I's inner circle.

While Osei Tutu I was in Akwamu, his uncle Obiri Yeboa succeeded King Oti Akenten and continued with Kwaman's conquest of new lands. In the early 1690s, King Obiri Yeboa died in battle with the Domaa, a neighboring state. The head of King Obiri Yeboa's household, Gyaasehene Adu Gyamfi, sent a delegation to Akwamu, requesting the return of Osei Tutu I to Kwaman to take King Obiri Yeboa's place.

CHAPTER 6

Osei Tutu I is King

Osei Tutu I prepared for his return to Kwaman. The King of Akwamu provided warriors for protection from Denkyira's forces, a gift of precious beads, and general supplies. On the way back, Osei Tutu I got smallpox, and his companions feared for his life. Who would dare report his death to the Gyaasehene? The men traveling with Osei Tutu I built him a separate hut, prepared cooked ground maize for his meals, and mashed plant bark for his skin. Osei Tutu I recovered after seven days and continued his journey.

On Osei Tutu I's arrival in Kwaman, the required period of mourning for King Obiri Yeboa was observed. The council of elders then started customary rites for his coronation (or enstoolment). Historians agree that by 1695, Osei Tutu I was King of Kwaman. King Osei Tutu I sent for his friend Firempong, now Okomfo Anokye, to assist him with the tasks at hand. King Osei Tutu I was keen to continue the work of his uncles, unifying the different Akan groups, knowing that only a powerful coalition could defeat Denkyira. The new king also vowed to punish Domaa for King Obiri Yeboa's death.

King Osei Tutu I planned to build military strength. This would give him authority to discuss forming a union with his peers, the kings of other Akan states. King Osei Tutu I reformed the military by creating eight units; Kontri, Benkum, Nifa, Adonten, Kyidom, Gyaase, Oyoko, and Akwamu. The Akwamu

contingent were the warriors who had traveled from Akwamu with the heir to the Kwaman throne, and only Oyoko clan members could join the Oyoko unit.

Another important change historians ascribe to King Osei Tutu I and his spiritual adviser is the change of name, from Kwaman to Kumasi. Asante lore tells that Okomfo Anokye planted seeds of what was known as the Kum tree in three locations: Kwaman, Kumawu, and Dwaben. The seedling in Kwaman survived and thus became known as *"kum-asi"* i.e., beneath the Kum tree. King Osei Tutu I was then no longer *Kwamanhene* (King of Kwaman) but *Kumasihene* (King of Kumasi).

CHAPTER 7

Early Victories

King Osei Tutu I, with an improved military, considered how to get cooperation from the strong states neighboring Kumasi, previously known as Kwaman. These states, Kaase, Amakom, Tafo, and Domaa, had threatened Kwaman's expansion plans for years. Both kings, Oti Akenten and Obiri Yeboa had tried and failed with military might, but King Osei Tutu I decided to use a give and take method.

The people of Kaase, southeast of Kumasi, were fierce and prized their independence. King Osei Tutu I took a wife from its royal family, giving him access to its organizational structures. He then used information gained to defeat Kaase, making it subordinate to his state. To foster a good relationship between Kumasi and Kaase though, he gave the Kaase king a role within Gyaasehene's unit. He turned his focus on the Amakom.

When the Oyoko arrived at Kwaman, as it was then known, the Amakom were already settled in the area. They grew into a large state to the east of Kumasi. King Osei Tutu I proposed marriage between his sister's daughter, Nyarko Kusi Amoa, and the Amakom king. This gave the people of Amakom a direct interest in the royal Oyoko house.

King Osei Tutu I, now with the backing of Kaase and Amakom, as well as the Gyaasehene, moved his troops into Tafo, located north of Kumasi. After the

conquest, King Osei Tutu I appointed the King of Tafo commander of the Kumasi Benkum unit. Tafo became a part of the Kumasi state.

Now, with this foundation, King Osei Tutu I prepared for an attack on Domaa. He successfully pushed Domaa further westward, away from Kumasi. However, these victories, as important as they were, did not give King Osei Tutu I the military strength to go against Denkyira. King Osei Tutu I was faced with the question of how to unify states located within the region, which included Dwaben, Nsuta, Kokofu, Bekwai, Mampong, and Asumengya. Could he get these kings to unify over their hatred of the yearly Denkyira tribute?

CHAPTER 8

Coalition Building

Around 1698, King Osei Tutu I was faced with increasing demands from the new King of Denkyira, Ntim Gyakari, who had succeeded Boa Amponsem in 1692. Ntim Gyakari noticed the growth of Kumasi and it displeased him. After all, Kumasi was a vassal state, and it must be reminded of its subordinate status. King Ntim Gyakari sent emissaries led by his shield-bearer, sword-bearer, and court crier to Kumasi. Ntim Gyakari demanded that King Osei Tutu I and his chiefs fill the large brass pan carried by the court crier with gold. In addition, the King and each of his chiefs must send his favorite wife to Denkyira.

When King Osei Tutu I and the other leaders resisted this unreasonable request, King Ntim Gyakari declared war. King Osei Tutu I and Okomfo Anokye saw an opportunity to unite the states. Not only were these states tired of Denkyira's disrespect, Nsuta, Dwaben, Kokofu, and Bekwai were founded by Oyoko clansmen. A meeting at Kumasi was called to discuss how to address King Ntim Gyakari's threat. The gathering included kings of the fellow Oyoko states and the King of Mampong, who belonged to a different clan.

According to local tradition, during the Friday gathering, Okomfo Anokye, the priest at the Kumasi royal court used magical powers to conjure a stool from the clouds. It descended and rested on King Osei Tutu I's lap. The priest

proclaimed that this was a divine selection of King Osei Tutu I or the occupant of the Kumasi stool as the leader of the military coalition formed. During a consecration ceremony led by Okomfo Anokye, after agreements were made, all the kings swore allegiance to the stool, named *Sika Dwa Kofi*, i.e., the Golden Stool known as Kofi. Okomfo Anokye presented the Golden Stool as the soul or unifying symbol of the coalition, known as Amantoo, with Kumasi as its capital. To ensure that no other stool had seniority to the Golden Stool, Okomfo Anokye took all other stools used in Kumasi and buried them at a secret spot in Bantama, the location in Kumasi where the meeting was held.

The King of Kumasi, as the leader of the coalition, would be the caretaker of the Golden Stool. The King of Mampong would be next in line, with his authority established by the Silver Stool. In the event King Osei Tutu I was unable to go to war, the King of Mampong became the commander of the union's army. The Golden Stool marked the beginning of a new type of union of Akan states. Whereas all traditional stools were black, this one was gold. The Amantoo coalition kings were now bound to fight as one nation, to retain their independence, and, to preserve the Golden Stool.

CHAPTER 9

War with Denkyira

King Osei Tutu I and the union prepared for war with Denkyira. He sent emissaries to Elmina to purchase arms and other war supplies. King Osei Tutu I continued to seek support from others oppressed by Denkyira. Many states joined the war on the union's side or at least allowed union forces and supplies to pass through their territories. They were tired of the King of Denkyira's taxes; the more the kings complied, the more Denkyira demanded.

To defend Amantoo, the union was divided into five military units: Adonten, Kyidom, Benkum, Nifa, and Gyaase. These were all led by kings of Amantoo states, except Gyaase. The Gyaasehene commanded the Gyaase, guard for the Kumasi King, Osei Tutu I. The *Mamponghene*, the second-in-command of Amantoo served as commander of Nifa, the right wing. The *Asumengyahene* commanded Benkum, the left wing. The Kumasi *Adontenhene*, on a level like the king or chief of a state, commanded the Adonten, the frontline of the Amantoo forces. Other kings and chiefs were appointed to positions within the various units and reported to wing commanders during the war.

The Amantoo war arrangement looked like an airplane. There was a central long column of scouts, followed by the Adonten, and then the commander-in-chief and his warriors. Facing the opposition direction was Kyidom, the rear unit. This column was supported by Nifa and Benkum wings. Each unit

had assistants including medical personnel. King Osei Tutu I designed the positioning of the Amantoo forces based on what he learned from the Denkyira and Akwamu military organizations.

By 1700, the war between Amantoo and Denkyira was fierce. It went on for two years with both sides suffering great losses. King Osei Tutu I knew that Amantoo had to succeed at all costs, as the wrath of Denkyira was known in the region. King Ntim Gyakari, on the other hand, believed that his forces were far superior to the union's army, paying no attention to the advances Amantoo made. At the battle of Feyiase, a few miles from Kumasi, King Osei Tutu I's unified forces defeated the fearsome Denkyira warriors.

It is said that the words that led to the name Asante came from Ntim Gyakari after his capture by Amantoo forces. Facing the fall of Denkyira, he cried, *"esa nti"* meaning, because of war. In his sorrow, Ntim Gyakari realized that the union had formed just to wage war with Denkyira. The Amantoo army marched to Denkyira's capital and gathered all Abankeseso's gold and wealth for the victorious army's return to Kumasi. The region was finally free from the oppressive shackles of Denkyira.

Amantoo War Arrangement

- Scouts
- Benkum — Left Wing
- Adonten — Forward Guard
- Nifa — Right Wing
- Gyaase — King's Guard
- Kyidom — Rear Guard

CHAPTER 10

The Asante Constitution

The fall of Denkyira led to the birth of the new Kingdom, Asante. However, King Osei Tutu I faced a major problem, keeping the coalition together. These were independent states that had unified for a single cause. They needed a bond beyond the desire to defeat a common enemy. What was the solution? King Osei Tutu I established a constitution for the new nation of Asante, which still exists today.

The Asante constitution appoints the *Asantehene* (also Kumasihene) as head of the nation, and the Mamponghene as second-in-command. It is said the Asantehene holds the head of the nation, and the Mamponghene, the nation's legs. The various kings of individual states or paramount chiefs, known collectively as *amanhene*, swear an oath of allegiance to the Asantehene when crowned or enstooled. In matters related to war and peace, the Asantehene has primary responsibility but considers advice from his amanhene. During war, each state brings soldiers who are placed in various army divisions. In individual states, though, it is the king (or paramount chief) who has primary responsibility and is assisted by a council of elders. A sub-chief in each state swears allegiance to his immediate king.

To assist the Asantehene, King Osei Tutu I created administrative groups. The Asanteman Council, led by the Asantehene and consisting of the amanhene,

serves like a legislative body. The Kumasi Council serves the Asantehene and is focused on matters relating to the state of Kumasi. The Asantehene, some amanhene, and the Kumasi Council form the Kotoko Council, a smaller inner circle. To help those states far away from Kumasi, King Osei Tutu I created the system of *Adamfo* that paired kings with a chief within Kumasi who helped with access to the Asantehene.

King Osei Tutu I desired to balance the power of the amanhene because these could easily upset the leadership structure. First, when new lands were acquired, King Osei Tutu I appointed members of the Kumasi division to govern these areas. Second, King Osei Tutu I created service stools where he rewarded faithful service with chiefdoms, moving leaders from the Gyaase division to these new positions or stools. Some records note that King Osei Tutu I assigned as many as thirty-one service chiefdoms or stools. New stools included the *Sannaahene* (chief of the king's treasury), *Adwumfohene* (chief of the guilds for skilled workers), and A*sokwa Batahene,* (chief of the traders). These were like ministers in a government Cabinet. Third, the role of the queen mother was officially recognized and Nyarko Kusi Amoa, daughter of King Osei Tutu I's aunt held the position.

Asante Leadership Chart and Councils

- **Asantehene (Kumasihene)**
- **Mamponghene (Second-in-Command)**
- **Amanhene (Kumasi) (Paramount Chiefs)**
- **Amanhene (Others) (Paramount Chiefs)**
- **Sub-Chiefs**
-  Adamfo

- **Asanteman Council (Legislature)** — Asantehene and amanhene
- **Kumasi Council** — Asantehene and Kumasi amanhene
- **Kotoko Council** — Asantehene, amanhene, and Kumasi council

CHAPTER 11

The Great King Dies

King Osei Tutu I planned to subdue another defiant state, Akyem. Akwamu and Akyem were old enemies. Akwamu had blocked Akyem's access to the coastal trade forcing Akyem to depend on Akwamu traders. So, when Akwamu and Asante built up a friendship, Akyem realized that this would make its coastal trading more difficult. How did Akyem respond? Akyem joined Denkyira in fighting against King Osei Tutu I and his coalition army. On Denkyira's defeat, Asante invaded Akyem and imposed a yearly tribute. However, Akyem rebelled against King Osei Tutu I by joining up with the remnant of Denkyira to regain Denkyira's lost status.

When Akyem continually failed to pay its tribute, King Osei Tutu I decided in 1717 to end Akyem's defiance. King Osei Tutu I sent his army on a march to Akyem. He would catch up with his troops after a trip to honor the memory of his predecessors. As King Osei Tutu I crossed the Pra River towards the war front, Akyem warriors lying in wait opened fire. The first round of fire on King Osei Tutu I and his troops left him wounded. King Osei Tutu I fell out of his hammock, trying to recover, but he was killed by a second shot.

King Osei Tutu I had misjudged the determination of the Akyem. He expressed regret with his last words, *"ankah me nim ma,"* meaning, if only I had known. The great founder of Asante fell into the river and his body was washed away.

There was widespread shock and mourning in Asante when news of his death reached the various parts of the nation. The grief made deeper because there was no body for burial. Many wondered if the new Kingdom of Asante would outlive its founding king. Yes, the union survived the death of King Osei Tutu I with his successor, continuing to expand its borders.

CHAPTER 12

King Osei Tutu I's Legacy

Through the war with Denkyira, King Osei Tutu I acquired the note on Elmina Castle and the Dutch traders transferred rent payments to Asante. The European traders were so fearful of this rising nation that had defeated Denkyira, the Dutch sent an emissary to Kumasi laden with gifts. This led to a relationship between the Asante, the people of Elmina, and Dutch traders and gave Asante direct access to the coastal trade. King Osei Tutu I's conquests continued, with victories in the west, taking Sefwi, Awowin, Wassa, and Apollonia around 1715.

King Osei Tutu I needed to encourage healthy relationships between members of the union. He established an annual festival where all the amanhene and their sub-chiefs came together; members should come together for reasons other than war. During the festival, dead chiefs were honored, forgiveness for past offenses sought and granted, and disputes between members settled. King Osei Tutu I required that all amanhene and sub-chiefs travel to Kumasi for the celebration. Kings and chiefs who did not attend had to provide a strong explanation for their absence. King Osei Tutu I prohibited public discussions of ancestry, which highlighted differences and led to disputes. Defeated kings and chiefs had to make regular visits to Kumasi to learn national traditions and history, and their heirs were required to spend time at King Osei Tutu I's court, much like he had done in Denkyira.

King Osei Tutu I transformed the small state of Kumasi, once known as Kwaman, at the mercy of the mighty elephants of Denkyira, into the capital of a union of Akan groups. He reformed the military and added service stools to reward faithful service, applying leadership skills he learned during his stay in Denkyira and Akwamu. He created a centralized government structure and expanded the boundaries of the nation. He built a trading system and placed Kumasi at its center, in addition to gaining access to important trade routes to the coast in the south, and to the north of the kingdom.

At his death in 1717, King Osei Tutu I's reputation had spread to other parts of West Africa, and he was recognized by European traders. King Osei Tutu I's reign helped to establish the Royal House of Oyoko as the only rightful heir to the Asante throne. The death of King Osei Tutu I is still remembered in a national oath, and the occupier of the Golden Stool is not allowed to cross the Pra River. Maanu Kotosii's son became a man of enormous influence, as predicted by the large Momordica that grew out of his discarded bathing sponge.

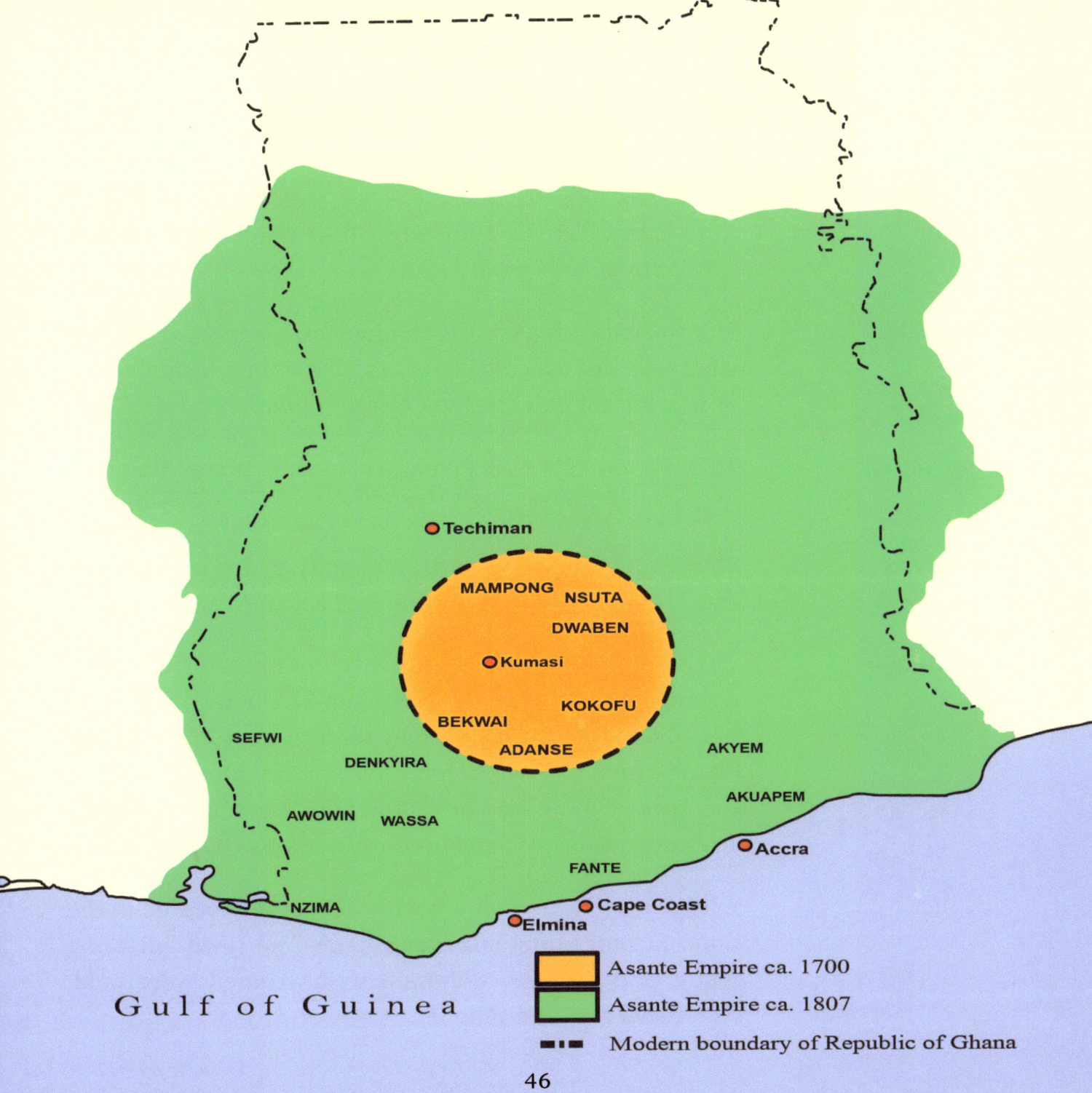

Glossary

Afuo	Afuo is the Twi word for farm. Twi, a dialect of Akan, is spoken by people from Asante.
Amanhene	The various kings of individual states or paramount chiefs are known collectively as amanhene. A single king or paramount chief is known as an *omanhene*.
Appellation	This is a name or title given to someone. It is often given with sound and rhyme.
Asante	The Asante (or Ashanti) are native to present-day south-central Ghana. They speak Twi, an Akan dialect.
Asantehene	The Asantehene is the King (or Paramount Chief) of Asante. A paramount chief has several sub-chiefs who report to him. Use of the word chief may refer to a paramount chief or sub-chief. The Asantehene, paramount chief or king of the Asante union also holds the position of Kumasihene. The current Asantehene is Otumfuo Nana Osei Tutu II.
Begho	A large ancient town known for its market, located in the Bono Region of modern-day Ghana. The town fell along many trade routes. Common items traded were gold, ivory, kola nut, and salt.

Denkyira	A strong Akan kingdom founded in the 1500s by the Agona clan in the southwestern area of modern-day Ghana. The capital city then was Abankeseso.
Emissary	This is a person sent as a representative of a state, government, or other entity.
Enstoolment	In the Akan tradition, when kings or chiefs are appointed, the ceremony is known as enstoolment, like being enthroned. The Akan king sits on a stool, regarded as his throne or the source of his authority.
Hene	The suffix "hene" means king or chief of the state to which it refers. For example, the Asantehene is the King of Asante.
Kum tree	Sources are unclear on the type of plant. Some claim cuttings of the Wawa or Ankye (or ackee) common in West Africa were planted. Others point to a banyan with roots that grow on the plant above the surface of the soil. The least likely suggestion is the black plum (Syzygium cumini) because it is distributed in Asian countries.
Kumasi	Previously known as Kwaman, it became the capital of the Asante Kingdom. Most writers give credit to King Osei Tutu I and Okomfo Anokye for the name change. However, others note that the change occurred as far back as King

	Oti Akenten's reign, when elders sat under a Kum tree to discuss issues of importance to the community.
Matrilineal	This is when the right of inheritance or ancestry passes through maternal lines.
Oware	A board game played by two. The board has hallowed out pits set in two parallel rows of six. The game begins with four pebbles in each pit and the objective is for a player to capture more pebbles than his (or her) opponent.
Oyoko	This is one of the major Akan clans. In Akan culture, a clan (or abusua) refers to a group of people with the same maternal ancestor. Other primary Akan clans are: Aduana, Agona, Asakyiri, Asnie, Asona, Bretuo, and Ekuona.
Sapɔ (or sponge)	Bathing sponge made from the thick stem of the tropical climbing plant called the *Momordica augustisepala* Harms. Its stem is beaten to a pulp and washed to remove impurities. The remaining whitish fibers are used as a sponge after drying.

Quiz

1. Which king first settled the Oyoko in Kwaman?
   - (a) Kwabia Anwanfi
   - (b) King Obiri Yeboa
   - (c) King Osei Tutu I
   - (d) King Oti Akenten

2. What was the name of King Osei Tutu I's mother?
   - (a) Maanu Kotosii
   - (b) Nyarko Kusi Amoa
   - (c) Ankyewaa Nyame
   - (d) Birepomaa Piesie

3. Which kingdom was Kwaman's overlord?
   - (a) Akwamu
   - (b) Denkyira
   - (c) Akyem
   - (d) Asantemanso

4. Where did King Osei Tutu I's coalition force defeat the mighty Kingdom of Denkyira?
   - (a) War of Adanse
   - (b) Battle at Kokofu
   - (c) Battle of Feyiase
   - (d) War at Akyem

Quiz Answers: DABC

References

Stoeltje, Beverly J. "Asante Queen Mothers in Ghana." *Oxford Research Encyclopedia of African History*. March 25, 2021. Oxford University Press. Date of access 6 Jul. 2023, https://oxfordre.com/africanhistory/view/10.1093/acrefore/9780190277734.001.0001/acrefore-9780190277734-e-796.

McCaskie, Tom. "Unspeakable Words, Unmasterable Feelings: Calamity and the Making of History in Asante." *Journal of African History*, vol. 59, no. 1, March 2018, https://doi.org/10.1017/S0021853717000408. Accessed 18 Jul. 2023.

Gedzi, Victor S. "The Asante of Ghana." *International Journal of African Society Cultures and Traditions*, vol.2, no. 3, December 2014, pp. 20-26.

Boakye, Emmanuel Osei. *Documentation and Dynamics of Oyoko Clan in Asante: Myth, Folklore and Meaning*. 2013. University of Ghana, MA dissertation.

McCaskie, T.C. "Denkyira in the Making of Asante, 1660-1720." *Journal of African History*, vol. 48, 2007, pp. 1-25.

Kaminski, Joseph S. "Asante Ivory Trumpets in Time, Place, and Context: An Analysis of a Field Study." *Historical Brass Journal*, vol. 15, 2003, doi: 10.2153/0120030011008. Accessed 14 Jul. 2023.

Prempeh I, and A. Adu. Boahen. *"The History of Ashanti Kings and the Whole Country Itself" and Other Writings / by Otumfuo, Nana Agyeman Prempeh I;*

Edited by A. Adu Boahen ... *[et Al.]*. Published for the British Academy by Oxford University Press, 2003.

Darkwah, Kofi. "Antecedents of Asante Culture." *Transactions of the Historical Society of Ghana*, New Series, no. 3, 1999, pp. 57-79.

McCaskie, Tom. "Komfo Anokye of Asante: Meaning, History and Philosophy in an African Society." *The Journal of African History*, vol. 27, no. 2, 1986, pp. 315-339.

Aidoo, Agnes A. "Order and Conflict in the Asante Empire: A Study in Interest Group Relations." *African Studies Review*, vol. 20, no. 1, April 1977, pp. 1-36.

Daaku, K. Yeboa. *Osei Tutu of Asante*. Heinemann, 1976.

Adu Boahen, A. "When Did Osei Tutu Die?" *Transactions of the Historical Society of Ghana*, vol. 16, no. 1, June 1975, pp. 87-92.

Anti, A.A. *Akwamu Denkyira Akuapem and Ashanti in the lives of Osei Tutu and Okomfo Anokye*. Ghana Publishing Corporation, 1971.

Fynn, John K. "Okomfo Anokye." *Encyclopedia Africana Dictionary of African Biography*, Volume 1, Ethiopia – Ghana, edited by L.H. Ofosu-Appiah, Reference Publications Inc., 1977, p. 286.

Fynn, John K. "Opoku Ware." *Encyclopedia Africana Dictionary of African Biography*, Volume 1, Ethiopia – Ghana, edited by L.H. Ofosu-Appiah, Reference Publications Inc., 1977, pp. 288-289.

Fynn, John K. "Osei Tutu." *Encyclopedia Africana Dictionary of African Biography*, Volume 1, Ethiopia – Ghana, edited by L.H. Ofosu-Appiah, Reference Publications Inc., 1977, pp. 294-295.

Arhin, Kwame. "The Structure of Greater Ashanti (1700-1824)." *The Journal of African History*, vol. 8, no. 1, 1967, pp. 65-86.

Meyerowitz, Eva L.R. "A Note on the Early History of the Jamasi People." *Transactions of the Gold Coast and Togoland Historical Society*, vol. 1, no. 4, 1955, pp. 141-143.

Fun Fact About the Asante

People of Asante shake hands in a unique way. This is because the Asante warrior holds a shield in his left hand and a spear in his right hand. The spear is to attack (offense), and the shield is for protection (defense). If the Asante warrior shakes your hand, it indicates trust. This is because to do so, the Asante warrior puts down his shield, his form of protection, and holds out his left hand for a handshake. However, if he misjudged the situation, he still has his right hand armed with his spear for protection. This way, the Asante warrior is not caught off guard.

Other Books in the Heritage Collection

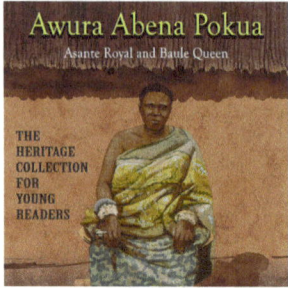
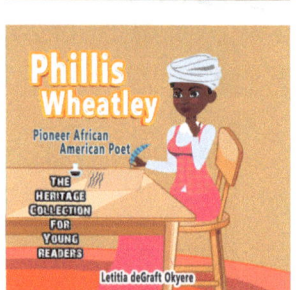

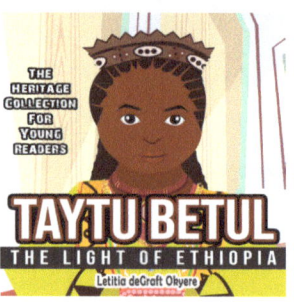

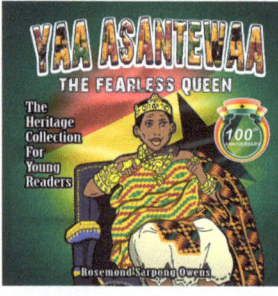
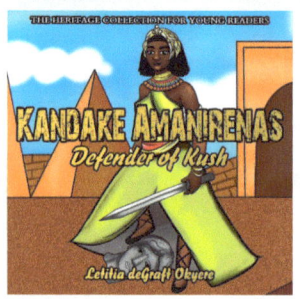
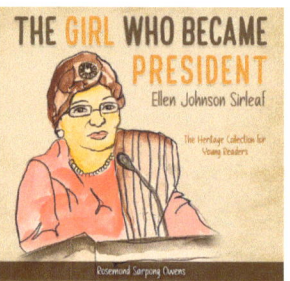

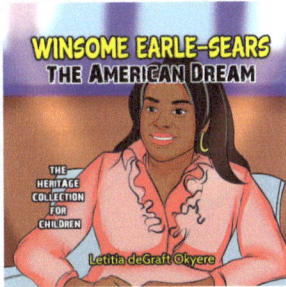

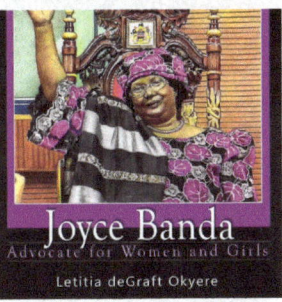
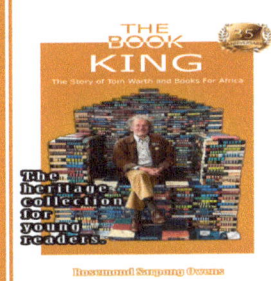

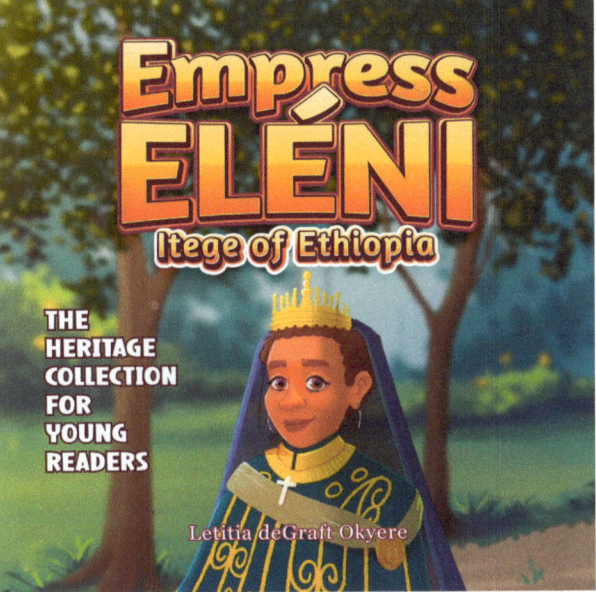
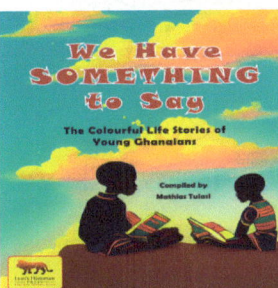
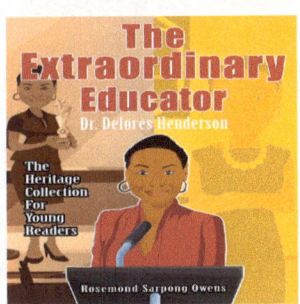